395

1. *Gate of Heavenly Peace* (T'ien-an Men), symbol of Peking and silent witness to the violent changes marking China's history. This famous gate was erected early in Ming times and later, in 1651, rebuilt in its present form. When demonstrations occur, the plaza in front of the gate becomes a sea of people topped by waves of red flags.

2. *Ch'iung-hua Island* in North Lake (Pei Hai) Park, originally part of an imperial garden but today a favorite place for relaxation. At the southern end of the lake, the island has unusual rock formations and a number of interesting structures, the largest of which is the Islamic tower (*dagoba*), a gleaming edifice built during the Ch'ing dynasty.

THIS BEAUTIFUL WORLD VOL. 3

PEKING

by HIKOTARŌ ANDŌ

 KODANSHA INTERNATIONAL LTD.
TOKYO, NEW YORK & SAN FRANCISCO

Distributors:
UNITED STATES: *Kodansha International/USA, Ltd., through Harper & Row, Publishers, Inc., 10 East 53rd Street, New York, New York 10022.* SOUTH AMERICA: *Harper & Row, Publishers, Inc., International Department.* CANADA: *Fitzhenry & Whiteside Limited, 150 Lesmill Road, Don Mills, Ontario.* MEXICO AND CENTRAL AMERICA: *HARLA S. A. de C. V., Apartado 30–546, Mexico 4, D. F.* UNITED KINGDOM: *Phaidon Press Limited, Littlegate House, St. Ebbe's Street, Oxford OX1 1SQ.* EUROPE: *Boxerbooks Inc., Limmatstrasse 111, 8031 Zurich.* AUSTRALIA AND NEW ZEALAND: *Book Wise (Australia) Pty. Ltd., 104–8 Sussex Street, Sydney 2000.* THE FAR EAST: *Toppan Company (S) Pte. Ltd., Box 22 Jurong Town Post Office, Jurong, Singapore 22.*

Published by Kodansha International Ltd., 2-12-21 Otowa, Bunkyo-ku, Tokyo 112 and Kodansha International/USA, Ltd., 10 East 53rd Street, New York, New York 10022 and 44 Montgomery Street, San Francisco, California 94104. Copyright © 1968 by Kodansha International Ltd. All rights reserved. Printed in Japan.

LCC 68–17459
ISBN 0–87011–060–8
JBC 0325–780590–2361

First edition, 1968
Seventh printing, 1977

Publisher's Note

PROFESSOR Andō is one of the few foreigners with a fluent grasp of the written and spoken Chinese language to have spent a protracted period of time in Peking during the present administration. His stay there has added significance because it coincided with the first formal stirrings of the Great Cultural Revolution and the Red Guards. Professor Andō's writings are interesting for several reasons: many of his comments are the result of first-hand contact with conditions in Peking, while his views on the Communist rule, although somewhat divergent with interpretations presently current in the West, are representative of many of his contemporaries in Japan.

Peking—A View from Japan comprises the section of the Japanese-language edition of *Peking* that deals with the city proper, excerpts from the author's article "My Two Years in Peking," which appeared in Vol. XIV, No. 1, of the *Japan Quarterly*, and some new additions prepared especially for this book. The publisher wishes to express its appreciation to the Asahi Shimbun Publishing Company for permission to use the excerpts from the *Japan Quarterly*. The opinions expressed in *Peking—A View from Japan* are entirely the author's.

CONTENTS

Preface

CHINA, like the sphinx of Egypt, has always been an enigma to the world. A land of complex mystery, China occupies one-fifth of the Asian continent and supports the world's largest population. Geographically, China has been separated from Europe by vast distances and the semi-arid plains to the west and north, from Southeast Asia by high mountains and jungles, and from Japan and the Americas by the Pacific Ocean. Today, modern transportation and communications have broken these ancient barriers, only to have them replaced by the new yet equally formidable barrier of a communist ideology blended with a unique cultural consciousness. Thus, despite its ancient civilization and great cultural heritage, China still stands alone among the major nations as unfathomable, as a country little known and even less understood.

Although China's culture had a significance in Asia analogous with that of Greece and Rome in ancient Europe, China has not receded into historical oblivion as its European counterparts did centuries ago. It still plays a significant role on the world stage today, with its influence being felt even beyond Asia. This new importance has grown increasingly since the founding of the People's Republic of China in 1949. But the puzzle of China has,

if anything, become even more difficult to solve. A new revolutionary rationale has been superimposed upon an old racial and cultural consciousness.

As a race, the Chinese are noted for their tenacity, a characteristic that has made it possible for them to avoid cultural assimilation by successive waves of invaders down through the centuries. China has tended, in fact, to absorb its invaders. And in modern times, it has been this cultural tenacity that has prevented both democracy and communism from being accepted in their alien form. China does not have a tradition of succumbing to alien ideologies. Although China has been "invaded" by foreign powers, it has never been "conquered," militarily or culturally, in modern times.

Since the founding of the People's Republic of China in 1949, however, China has been looked upon by the world, particularly the West, as a growing monster of obscure character. As the bitter enemy of "American imperialism" and a heretic in the communist camp, China has become an international loner. But with its large land territory and huge population, it is, in itself, a universe. To ignore these facts is a fatal mistake.

Although the whole of China cannot be understood by knowing Peking, the capital, it is impossible to understand China without knowing this ancient city. In certain respects, it is like Washington, London, and Paris. In other respects it is similar to Moscow, the center of international communism, and to the Vatican, the center of Catholicism. Yet it is its own unique self.

The Great Cultural Revolution focused world attention again on Peking in 1966. Organizing themselves as the Red Guards, the young people of the city suddenly shook and loosened the iron

discipline of the Chinese Communist Party and government organizations. The movement spread swiftly throughout China, and the old image of solidarity was broken. Even today the significance of this event is still not clear, adding further to the Chinese puzzle.

But no matter how enigmatic China and its capital of Peking may appear, the people there do not really think and live in ways that are completely different from the past—nor are their basic human needs and desires so different from those found among other peoples throughout the world. Asian mystery, compounded by revolutionary communism, presents an image to the world that makes China difficult for Westerners to approach. And because it is difficult to comprehend, it becomes something fearful. The reverse, however, is also true. If its nature is understood correctly, something fearful can be approached and can even be intimately known.

The daily life of the people of Peking is surprisingly ordinary. It is lived, of course, under the rules of a socialistic country, but many old habits and customs are retained: an afternoon nap after lunch, for instance. Even university professors still indulge in this custom, a situation that may strike us as humorous. No matter what their stations in life, the people have the right to a minimum of health and culture. In China the means toward realizing this end may differ from that in other countries, but to differ is not necessarily to err. It must be recognized by the people of the West that there is more than one way of achieving these objectives.

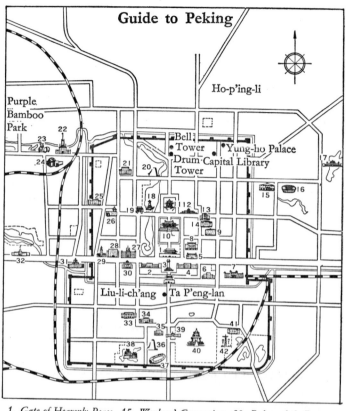

Guide to Peking

Ho-p'ing-li

Purple Bamboo Park

Bell Tower

Yung-ho Palace

Drum Tower

Capital Library

Liu-li-ch'ang • Ta P'eng-lan

1. Gate of Heavenly Peace
2. People's Assembly Hall
3. Heroes Memorial
4. Museum of History
5. Peking Hotel
6. New China Hotel
7. Peking Station
8. Peking Dept. Store
9. Amity Guest House
10. Old Palace
11. Prospect Hill
12. Museum of Art
13. China Hotel
14. Capital Theater

15. Workers' Gymnasium
16. Workers' Stadium
17. Agricultural Exhibit
18. North Lake Park
19. Peking Library
20. Shih-cha-hai Pool
21. People's Theater
22. Peking Exhibit Hall
23. Peking Zoo
24. Peking Observatory
25. Lu Hsun Museum
26. Geological Museum
27. Telegraph Office
28. Int'l. Travel Agency

29. Palace of the Races
30. Capital Movie Theater
31. Peking Radio Building
32. Military Museum
33. Peking Workers' Club
34. Ch'ien-men Restaurant
35. T'ien-ch'iao Theater
36. T'ou-jan-t'ing Pool
37. Hsien-nung-t'an Stadium
38. T'ou-na-t'ing Park
39. Natural Science Museum
40. T'ien-t'an Park
41. Peking Gymnasium
42. Parachute Tower

3. *Corner tower of the Old Palace*, reflected in the waters of a moat, is a reminder of the colorful past of imperial China. Formerly called the Forbidden City, the home of the Ming and Ch'ing emperors, the Old Palace is situated in the heart of Peking. Once the scene of countless intrigues, these walls now house a museum.

PEKING

Fo-hsiang Pavilion in I-ho Park, a popular sight-seeing spot in the northwestern suburbs of Peking. Situated atop Wan-shou Hill, this structure stands some 150 feet high and commands a fine view of K'un-ming Lake. Although it originally had nine tiers, the pavilion was shortened to four tiers during the Ch'ing dynasty.

Peking

A View from Japan

AT THREE o'clock on October 1, 1949, Mao Tse-tung proclaimed in his characteristically shrill voice the establishment of the Chinese People's Republic. On that day, tens of thousands of people gathered in front of the Gate of Heavenly Peace, but the square at the time was still surrounded by a palace wall built in the time of the Mings and was only one-fifth its present size. Moreover, since it was immediately after the revolution, transportation systems were still inadequate, so that students of Ch'ing-hua University in the western suburbs had to rise at five in the morning to get to the gate on time. Following the three o'clock declaration, they formed a parade and marched back to their school, arriving there at two o'clock the next morning. Today, special buses provide round-trip transportation from distant spots for celebrations.

The legal basis for the ceremony establishing the new nation was formulated in September of the same year at a meeting of the Chinese People's Political Consultative Conference. At six p.m. on September 30, the final day of this conference, which was attended by various democratic parties and independent progressives, Mao Tse-tung appeared personally at the Gate of Heavenly Peace to take the first symbolic step in constructing a new nation, laying the cornerstone for a structure that today towers high above the center of the square—the Memorial to the People's Heroes. This memorial is made of granite and stands some 128 feet high on a base some ten thousand square feet in area. The face bears an inscription, in Mao's hand: "The People's Heroes Will Be Remembered Eternally." On the back of the monument are inscribed, in Chou En-lai's writing, words of tribute to those who sacrificed themselves for the sake of national independence and peace from the time of the Opium War until the present. Around the base of the tower are eight reliefs depicting scenes from the Opium War, the May 4 Movement, and other events in revolutionary history. Although the cornerstone was laid in 1949, actual work did not begin until three years later and the monument was not completed until May Day in 1958. Beside the square, flanking the monument, stand the Chinese People's Revolution and History museums on the east and the People's Assembly Hall on the west. These were also completed in 1958, when the square first attained its present size. The People's Assembly Hall has, in addition to a conference hall with a capacity of ten thousand people, a huge banquet hall seating five thousand and other rooms with folk-art decorations and furniture from Kiangsi, Szechuan, and other provinces. Altogether, the building will hold some forty thousand people. Held here are meetings of the Assembly of People's Representatives as well as other mass meetings.

The museums of History and the Chinese People's Revolution, are located to the right and left of a central arcade and courtyard, the Chinese People's Revolution Museum standing closer to the Gate of Heavenly Peace. The final exhibit one sees in the latter is a high red flag with five stars. It is the flag that flew over the

Gate of Heavenly Peace on October 1, 1949, and is an emotion-charged symbol of over one hundred years of struggle for independence and freedom. It is before this flag that children take the oath when joining the Pioneers, a Communist organization for elementary school children, and one often sees them solemnly raising their small fists in front of it. The People's Assembly Hall, a modern building topped with a traditional tiled roof, and the museums of History and the Chinese People's Revolution face each other across the square. In the center to the south stands the Memorial to the People's Heroes, and through the green pines behind it can be seen the towering Cheng-yang Gate, the entrance to the inner city. Facing north in front of the Memorial, one can see the massive vermilion-painted structure of the Gate of Heavenly Peace. It is a typical example of Chinese architecture, which characteristically hugs the earth, as though it had put down roots, rather than towering high in the sky. Immediately in front of the Gate of Heavenly Peace is a moat, spanned by a bridge of marble; anyone may cross it and pass through the gate, to where the palaces of the old imperial families stand.

Stretching out to the east and west from the Gate of Heavenly Peace are two main streets, over three hundred feet in width, known as Tung-ch'ang-an (East Long Peace) and Hsi-ch'ang-an (West Long Peace). And on the north, i.e., in line with the gate, is a row of large buildings including the Cultural Palace of the Races, the Peking Telegraph Office, and the Peking Hotel.

During celebrations of National Foundation Day on the 1st of October, portraits of Mao Tse-tung are strung across the Gate of Heavenly Peace, a huge portrait of Sun Yat-sen is mounted on the Memorial facing the gate, portraits of Marx and Engels are mounted on the museum side (that is, on Tung-ch'ang-an Street), and huge portraits of Lenin and Stalin on Hsi-ch'ang-an Street. The lines connecting the portraits of Marx, Engels, Lenin, and those connecting Mao Tse-tung and Sun Yat-sen, cross precisely over the square—a detail that is symbolic of the Chinese apprehension of history. The gate of Heavenly Peace and the square in front of it, with their harmonious blend of the traditional and the new, are also a fitting symbol of the capital of the revolution, Peking—indeed, of all China.

On August 18, 1966, one million people gathered before the Gate of Heavenly Peace to celebrate the Great Proletarian Cultural Revolution. Mao Tse-tung, Lin Piao, Chou En-lai, and many other leaders ascended the gate to receive the cheers of the chanting throng. It was from this moment that the Red Guards came to attract the attention of the outside world.

Since all central political and cultural agencies are in Peking, revolutionary activities affecting not only the city but the whole nation are concentrated here. Gatherings of a million Red Guards subsequently occurred on several occasions in the square before the Gate of Heavenly Peace, and young people from all parts of China came on foot and by train to take part.

The emergence of the Red Guards came as a great surprise in Japan and reports all spoke as though something rather shocking had happened. But in fact, to someone inside Peking, it was neither unexpected nor incomprehensible.

The Socialist Education Movement, which had been in progress in people's communes in rural communities all over the country since early 1963, was causing a fundamental upheaval in those communities because of its drive—known as the "Four Purifications Movement" —to clean up their political, ideological, organizational and economic life. The poor and lower-middle echelon of farmers were being organized in a bitter struggle against "economism" (the policy of material reward) in the communes and "bureaucratism" in the leadership. The Great Cultural Revolution was launched on the basis of what had already been achieved by this movement. It was part of one great movement that for several years past had been spreading from the farms to the cities. It was Peking, the capital of the revolution, that served as a focal point where the achievements of the Socialist Education Movement were concentrated and reduced to their essence ready for re-dissemination throughout the nation again. When a reshuffle of the leaders of the Chinese Communist Party's Peking Municipal Committee who had followed the wrong road was announced on June 3, 1966, demonstrations in support of this move continued for several days. From then on, the struggle went ahead in workshops and schools, and a revolutionary organization known as the Red Guards was formed by the teachers and students of the universities and high schools. Eventually, by January of 1967, it developed into a "struggle to seize authority" and on the 20th of April, 1967, the Peking Municipal Revolutionary Committee was established as a source of authority in Peking. The Great Cultural Revolution in Peking was taken as a model for the entire country.

The Great Cultural Revolution seeks to demonstrate the possibility and necessity of revolution within a socialistic society. In a sense, it reveals previously existing historical and social concepts in an entirely new perspective. It only became possible on the basis of experience gained in socialist construction since the establishment of socialism in China in 1949. As socialist reconstruction began to succeed, varying underlying troublesome contradictions developed and there were subtle shifts in foreign relations, all of which led Mao Tse-tung to formulate his theories on "the correct handling of contradictions." In 1962, the theory of the class struggle in the transitional period was also formulated; these gave rise to the Socialist Education Movement, and eventually to the Great Cultural Revolution. From its strategic position in the center of Peking, the Gate of Heavenly Peace has been a silent observer of this process.

We have seen how the Great Proletarian Cultural Revolution had its first origins in the Socialist Education Movement, which was started among the farmers in order to foster a clear understanding of, and to overcome the contradictions arising in the process of establishing socialism. However, development of the Socialist Education Movement into a Great Cultural Revolution on a nationwide scale was a leap forward that required a prolonged stimulus to make it possible. This was found in a campaign of criticism leveled at Wu Han, a historian who was also Deputy Mayor of Peking.

On the 10th of November, 1965, an article by Yao Wen-yuang criticizing Wu Han appeared in Shanghai's *Wen Hui Pao* daily newspaper, and immediately provoked lively debate among the people. Criticism of Wu Han mounted progressively, and in March of 1966, with the reorganization of the Peking Municipal Committee and the dismissal of Peng Chen, the Mayor, the Cultural Revolution reached a peak of intensity.

The Great Cultural Revolution aimed, not only at rectifying

administrative and technical contradictions arising in the course of socialist construction, but also at getting rid of the so-called *ssu chiu* or "Four Olds": old ideas, old culture, old customs, and old ways. Elimination of these "Four Olds" necessitated not only rebellion against leaders who were following bureaucratic or mistaken courses, but also attack on such tendencies within the individual. This meant that it now became necessary to apply stricter standards of morality to social life and to relations between the sexes.

Although the Great Cultural Revolution made some progress in the workshops and among the people in general, its most dauntless champions were the Red Guards organized in the universities and high schools. Encouraged by the principle, "rebellion is justified," these young people expressed their opinions by sticking up wall posters, the so-called "big character newspapers" (although they are not really newspapers), throughout the city and changing any street names that brought to mind the old society.

Wang Fu-ching, Peking's main thoroughfare had its name changed to "People's Road," because its old name referred to the well of a feudal dictator. Similarly, the street formerly lined with the embassies of the "imperialistic" countries—Tung-chiao-min-hsiang, the street said to be barred to "dogs and Chinese"—was renamed "Anti-Imperialist Street." Peking was filled with youthful vigor. The demonstrations of the Great Cultural Revolution, unlike those of other countries, are noted for their noisy whistles and drums.

It was in front of the Gate of Heavenly Peace that the May 4 Movement of 1919 got under way and the December 9 Movement of 1935 unfolded. Both were started by young people, and, in the

21

PEKING 北京

Great Cultural Revolution, youth once more became the main driving force.

The city of Peking has a long and interesting history. Records show that four thousand years ago, in the time of T'ang Yu, there was already a town on the site of the present city of Peking by the name of Yu-chou, while three thousand years ago, during the Chou dynasty, the feudal state of Yen established a city in the same place and called it Chi Ch'eng.

It is said that this site was chosen for a capital by the Chin feudal state early in the Christian era. In 1263, the Mongols of the Yuan dynasty made it their capital, calling it "Great City" (Ta-tu), and began construction on a large scale. The Great City of the Mongols is believed to have lain somewhat north of the present palace.

In 1420, after the decline of the Yuan dynasty, the Ming, who had first established themselves at Nanking, moved their capital to Peking. It is from this time that the city was known as Peking. When the Ming dynasty was followed by the Ch'ing, the capital remained, additions being made to the foundations established by the Ming.

The Imperial City is located in the center of Peking, and in the
The Imperial City is located in the center of Peking, and in the
center of these palace grounds is the Forbidden City. Beyond the Gate of Heavenly Peace stands the Noon (Wu) Gate, and beyond that again lies the Forbidden City. The Ch'iang Wall running from the Gate of Heavenly Peace, originally skirted the outer boundaries, but only the section on the southern side, that is, the side of the Gate of Heavenly Peace, remains today. The other three sides were dismantled with the fall of the Ch'ing dynasty. Even today,

fragments of the large wall surrounding the palace grounds still remain in places between houses, a reminder of the vast scale of the old Imperial City.

In the center of the southern side of Peking's outer wall stood the Yung-ting (Eternal Stability) Gate (no traces remain today), and directly to the north of this lies the entrance to the inner city, Cheng-yang Gate. On the other side of this lies the Square and Gate of Heavenly Peace. Next comes the Tuan Gate and beyond it, Wu Gate, the entrance to the Forbidden City. One passes between the golden, shimmering buildings of the Forbidden City, and emerges at the Shen-Wu Gate on the far north side. Outside the Forbidden City on the north stands an artificial mount, Prospect Hill. From the Pavilion of Ten Thousand Springs (Wan-ch'un T'ing) on the summit of Prospect Hill, the Forbidden City and the entire Imperial City can be viewed. Beyond Prospect Hill on the north side of Peking once stood the Gate of Earthly Peace (Ti-an Men), which was torn down. Still further beyond stands the Drum Tower (Ku Lou), and behind it the Bell Tower (Chung Lou). The north-south axis from Yung-ting Gate in the south to the Bell Tower in the north, a distance of some five miles, forms the backbone of Peking.

To the west of the Forbidden City and Prospect Hill, extending in a chain from north to south, lie three connected lakes—North Lake, Central Lake, and South Lake. The first two date back to the ninth century, the last to the beginning of the Ming Period. The grounds of the South and Central lakes are now the site of a government office and are open to the public, but there is a view over both of them from the bridge over North Lake. The grounds of North Lake, a skillful combination of natural and artificial beauty, are now a park, and are crowded on Sundays with family groups. Peking, with its scanty rainfall, lies on the very edge of the dry wastes of Asia, and the construction of such a large lake in the city was a remarkable feat.

The Emperors of the feudal period prohibited two-story buildings for the ordinary people, so that the line of the eaves is low, and the rows of houses of gray brick, with roofs of tile, give Peking as a whole a somber, archaic air. As houses fall into disrepair they are torn down, and apartment houses of the type now mushrooming in the suburbs are put up in their place. Even so, the side streets with their stone paving still generate the old atmosphere, and the walls bordering them seem to be impregnated with the very history of the city.

The typical Peking residence encloses a square courtyard called *yüan-tzu*, which always has a south-facing gate. The main wing of the house also faces south, on the other side of the courtyard from the gate. In front of the gate stand pagoda trees, and in the courtyard are Chinese date or other species of trees. These residences make the city a forest of green when viewed from the top of Prospect Hill. Houses of this type are called *ssu-ho yüan*.

A typical *ssu-ho yüan* is the old home of Lu Hsun near F'ou-ch'ang Gate. He lived here for three years from September 1924; this was his residence when he participated in the March 18 Incident and when he wrote his famous "Rose Without a Flower," and the very walls seem to breathe the sorrow that he felt under the yoke of the government of the day. Nearby stands the Lu Hsun Museum. The former house of the famous painter of horses, Hsu Pei-hung, near Peking Station is also preserved and is open to the public.

⚑ A VIEW FROM JAPAN

The side streets of Peking have much to offer. Especially enjoyable is Liu-li Ch'ang, where antique shops, writing-brush shops, "chop" engraving shops, and old book shops crowd each other eave to eave. Few foreigners other than Japanese can be seen walking this street now—but then, other than Chinese, perhaps only Japanese would be interested in searching out an interesting stone for a "chop" in one of these shops.

Yet even here the fresh breeze of the new China is blowing. In the old days, valuable old books could be found as bargains in these shops, and foreigners would buy them and take them out of the country in great numbers. Today, the government buys all valuable books and puts them in museums and libraries, so there are few "finds" such as there were before the present government took over. For those who enjoy looking for bargains, this is a sad thing, but for China it is a very good thing.

Museums and libraries are among the new attractions of Peking. First and foremost, there are the Museum of History and the Museum of the People's Revolution on the east side of the square before the Gate of Heavenly Peace. These are not merely repositories of relics of civilization, but living institutions of education that are always crowded with visitors. Not only the young Pioneers, but also tourists who have come in groups to lay flowers at the Memorial to the Heroes of the Revolution come here to find fresh inspiration in their task of national reconstruction. The Museum of History contains items from the beginning of history down to the end of the Ch'ing dynasty, while the Museum of the People's Revolution covers the period from the Opium Wars down to the founding of the People's Republic.

Other museums include the Old Palace Museum, with its exhibits of ancient cultural objects, the Museum of Natural Science at the Bridge of Heaven outside the walls, with its rich collections of specimens of flora and fauna. The Astronomical Institute, complete with a planetarium, which stands outside Hsi-chih Gate; the Museum of Geology; the Lu Hsun Museum; the Hsu Pei-hung Memorial Hall—to visit only those museums within the city proper is quite a task.

Another building that may be included among the museums is the Cultural Palace of the Races, a structure built in the traditional style with a thirteen-tiered tower that reaches some 205 feet into the air, at West Ch'ang-an Street. In addition to the Han race, China has fifty-four racial minority groups within its borders, comprising six percent of the population, or about thirty-eight million people, scattered over approximately six percent of China's land area. Most of them in the past suffered under feudal systems or a primitive type of serfdom, but with the attachment of Tibet, the last remaining problem of this kind was solved. Exhibits in the Cultural Palace of the Races show in detail the history of these minorities as well as their present development. The Tibetan exhibit is particularly horrifying, showing eye-gouges and pillories used on tenants who failed to pay their rent.

The largest of the museums is the Military Museum of the Chinese People's Revolution outside Fu-hsing Gate, under the jurisdiction of the People's Liberation Army. Women guides are used in all Peking's museums, but in this museum they are army women. The museum has nine wings, devoted to the second Internal

Revolutionary War, the War Against Japan, the Third Internal Revolutionary War, the Defense of Socialist Construction, Aid to Korea Against the U.S., the militia, decorations, and general items. American planes shot down in Chinese territory are often displayed here, and draw large crowds.

Libraries include the famous Peking Library, which contains approximately ten million books stored in imposing Chinese-style stacks. There is also the Metropolitan Library, which contains some one million volumes, occupying the premises of the old Hall of Classics in the Tung-chi'eng district. The Hall of Classics during feudal times was the highest institute of learning; it was built by the Yüan dynasty in 1287. Today part of the building, together with the Mausoleum of Confucius on the west side, is used as a library, and the building itself is preserved in its original form.

Other large buildings in Peking are the huge Agricultural Exhibit Hall of China in the eastern suburbs, and the Museum of Chinese Art, with its golden-tiled roof, on Chu-shih Boulevard. Chinese-style structures built after the present government came to power, they are already well-known sightseeing places in Peking. Other famous places are the Peking Workers' Gymnasium and the Peking Workers' Stadium outside the Ch'ao-yang Gate. The former was completed in February of 1962 and has a capacity of fifteen thousand. The Stadium holds eighty thousand people, and often one hundred thousand people participate in demonstrations held here.

Two other famous places which deserve mention are the twin gateways to Peking: Peking Airport and Peking Station. Peking Airport is about twenty-five miles northeast of the city in Shun-i district. This was the site of a great battle during the last war between China and Japan, and the peasants dug tunnels here, from house to house and village to village, to enable resistance to be continued. Part of this "underground battlefield" can still be seen today. It is ironical that the first friendly greetings that Japanese visitors exchange with their hosts on arrival in Peking should take place on this site of old animosities.

Chinese newspapers always carry the date according to the old calendar. This is called either the "Hsia calendar," since it came into being under Emperor Yu of the ancient Hsia dynasty, or the "agricultural calendar." Originating with the ancient civilization of the Yellow River, it fits in admirably with the seasons. The "first day of spring" according to the old calendar is almost always warm, and rain really falls when it is supposed to. The "hottest day of summer" is really hot, and cool breezes rise at the official start of autumn. The "twenty-four periods" of a year are well organized and call forth our respect for the wisdom of the ancients.

For the citizens of Peking, what is known as "the turn of the year" does not normally refer to the New Year according to the new calendar, but to the "Spring Festival," the New Year by the old calendar. The New Year according to the new calendar rates a national holiday of one day, but the New Year of the old calendar rates a holiday of three days. Moreover, if this term includes a Sunday, the holiday stretches over four days. The Spring Festival is the time when the children get out their new clothes. In winter the people of Peking wear a Chinese-style garment, *men-ao*, a jacket padded with cotton. Beneath this, some wear the old cotton-padded trousers; others wear modern trousers. The *men-ao* is usually of dark blue cotton, but for special occasions women wear flowered silk. A single-layer, easily washable jacket with hooks instead of buttons is worn over the *men-ao*; at the Spring Festival the old jackets are usually changed for new.

National holidays are the three days of the New Year, the one day of the new-calendar New Year, May Day, and the anniversary of the founding day on October 1, which is a two-day holiday. In addition, students have a holiday from school at the "Youth Festival" on May 4, to celebrate the May 4 Movement, while on the 1st of August, soldiers of the People's Liberation Army celebrate the liberation. These last two are not general holidays.

Other days celebrated according to the old calendar are the 5th of May, Boys' Day, when special reed-wrapped dumplings are eaten, and the 15th of August, the Mid-Autumn Festival, when people eat "moon cookies" containing five different kinds of seed and go moon-viewing. On the latter occasion, large numbers of people throng North Lake Park and Prospect Hill to see the moon. At North Lake, floating musical concerts are held and the people rent boats to gather around the stage in the middle of the lake.

Even though the old calendar remains, the customs of visiting temples and holding religious ceremonies has disappeared. For example, the Ch'ing Ming festival, around the 5th of April by the new calendar, was formerly the day for visiting temples and the graves of ancestors. Now, this day is reserved for the offering of flowers at the People's Heroes Monument in the square of the Gate of Heavenly Peace and at the Cemetery for Revolutionary Warriors at Pa-pao Hill (Eight Treasures Hill) outside the Fu-hsing Gate.

Around the time of the Ch'ing Ming Festival, the base of the People's Heroes Memorial is smothered with wreathes of flowers. Large numbers of people approach in serried ranks and make pledges, and the "Internationale" is sung by choruses. When the strains of the "Internationale" are heard, one has the feeling that one is indeed in a revolutionary capital of the revolution.

This fashioning of new customs is part of deliberate policy to pour new wine into the old bottles of tradition. The 1st of March, May Day, and National Foundation Day on the 1st of October are new annual rites, and as such have already been accepted among the people, but particularly interesting are cases such as this Ch'ing Ming Festival where the form has been retained and the content changed. The Spring Festival in Peking is a similar case. It was formerly centered around a fair in the Liu-li Ch'ang, the book store area, with street stalls and surging crowds. The street stalls sold "New Year's" pictures, toys for children, and sugared sweet gourd (*t'ang hu-lu*) skewered on willow branches. Today, this fair and fête day atmosphere is no more. In the dusty streets of Peking in the winter, the long *t'ang hu-lu* had a tendency to get dirty, and they are now sold skewered on short bamboo splinters from glass-covered cases on street corners. Kites and Chinese tops are the same as they were in the past, but they are now sold at toy shops and not street stalls.

The "New Year's" pictures that featured the God of Good Fortune and were pasted on city walls have been replaced, needless to say, by revolutionary pictures depicting the joys of labor. Another result of the new policy is the marathon race around the city held on the last day of the Spring Festival, which has already become an eagerly awaited event. Thousands of young people start from the Gate of Heavenly Peace and run around a course of more than fifteen thousand yards that takes them out as far as Pei-hsin Bridge and then back to the starting point. The sight of these young people running this course in a temperature of more than ten degrees below zero is an accurate indication of the robustness of the new China.

Dawn breaks late in mid-winter Peking—around 7:30—so working hours usually start from nine o'clock, although the normal workday begins at eight o'clock in other seasons. Before setting off for work, or perhaps at a small snack bar along the way, the worker or student will have a simple breakfast of stuffed buns (*yu-ping*) or round wheat cakes (*shao-ping*). Sometimes the stuffed buns or long, narrow fried bread (*yu-t'iao*) are bought and eaten while walking to work. It is not unusual to see children eating their breakfast in this manner on their way to school.

Since it is common for both parents to have jobs in China, the first stop on the way to work is often at one of the many nurseries to leave off younger children. Although there are various types— some large factories and city communes operate their own, while municipal wards and individuals operate others—the nurseries run by the older people of the Neighborhood Committees (the lowest level of government administration) are most popular because of their convenience. At some nurseries, children will be looked after for the entire week, from Monday morning to Saturday afternoon, but most work on a daily basis or a combination of the two. The larger nurseries usually have trained supervisors.

Whether the working day starts at eight or nine o'clock, the worker can look forward to a fifteen minute rest period during mid-morning. This usually begins at ten o'clock, at which time music for calisthenics is broadcast over the shop radios. Some workers go out into the courtyard to exercise, others play volleyball

31

or other games, and still others practice the traditional martial art of *t'ai-chi ch'uan*. Exercise takes many forms, and strict conformity is not insisted on.

After lunch, according to the national custom, everyone takes a nap that lasts until 2:00 p.m. during the winter months, and 2:30 p.m. or 3:00 p.m. in the summer. Quiet reigns throughout the city, although the shops on main streets remain open and buses continue to operate. This custom of taking an afternoon nap has been unaffected even by the Great Cultural Revolution and, as a rule, the holding of street demonstrations at this time is avoided. Since it is common in China to live close to one's place of work, many people return home to nap; those who live far away usually stretch out on temporary cots in the shops. Even university professors and students follow this custom.

In the afternoon, there is another fifteen minute break at four o'clock, at which time music for calisthenics is again broadcast over the radio. The regular workday ends at six thirty, although in some factories there are several work shifts. According to policy, overtime work is avoided as far as possible. Excluding the exercise periods, the workday is seven and a half hours. This taking of afternoon naps and avoiding overtime work is known as the "principle of combined work and rest," a daily routine found not only in Peking but throughout China.

Many workers take their evening meal at the workshop. Sometimes, when a husband works at a different shop than his wife, both will meet at one shop for their evening meal, those with children bringing them along from the nursery. Often children, with red scarves tied around their necks, can be seen gathering noisily at workshops to meet their parents and to accompany them home for the evening meal. This meal, usually consisting of two or three dishes besides rice, comprises the main meal of the day. China's low prices will allow one person three meals a day for less than fifty cents.

Workers, however, occasionally take advantage of the many small drinking places in the evening, whether they eat at their place of work or at home. These small places, often the corner of a grocery store furnished with tables and chairs, serve simple appetizers to go with the drinks. Wine is the main beverage served at these *hsiao-ch'ih tien*, which are usually open between 8:00 and 11:00 p.m., and it is ordinarily drunk with a late evening meal or snack. A common scene in these popular shops is that of a husband and wife enjoying themselves, the former drinking wine and the latter eating *wonton*, a soup containing the Chinese version of ravioli. Low prices also account partly for the popularity of these shops. The local Chinese wine, *erh-kuo-t'ou*, sells for a little over ten cents a pint, and a side dish of pork in soybean paste costs about four cents. If the customer tipples too much, he can buy a bowl of *wonton* for about seven cents. Altogether, the whole evening in the shop may cost him about forty cents.

Those working couples who take their evening meals at home rather than at the workshop usually live with older family members. On occasion, they will also dine out family-style at one of the many and varied restaurants in the city. Almost any style of Chinese cooking can be found in Peking in addition to the rich native dishes of the city. Restaurants specializing in the dishes of Canton, Mongolia, Szechuan, and other areas of China are all represented. There is even a Japanese and several Western-style restaurants.

PEKING 火

Saturday evenings are most popular for these family dinners on the town, for that is the time when the children are home from the nurseries and other family members can be brought together easily.

Saturday evenings are also the busiest for the movie theaters, a common form of after-dinner entertainment. Peking movie houses sell only reserved seat tickets and, although cheap (the equivalent of about eleven cents), the tickets must be ordered in advance from union halls or booking agencies. Of all the traditional dramatic forms the motion-picture drama has borne the brunt of criticism since the start of the Great Cultural Revolution. But even those films which have been labelled "poisonous herbs"—as an indication of the moral standard of their content—are still shown. Considered paradoxical teaching material, they are given as an example of what *not* to do. Paradoxically, these "poisonous herbs" are the only dramatic films being shown in Peking at present. Production of films with normal moral themes has come to a temporary halt, and until production is resumed, their place has been taken in the theaters by news documentaries.

Another form of entertainment is the traditional theater of Peking. Here reforms have been completed. Probably the most representative of Peking's traditional plays was the type known as *Chin-chui*, with a history of three hundred years. Gripped by a feudalistic teacher-pupil relationship, the theatrical groups clung to the old interpretaions and gradually the theater became so removed from reality as to become unintelligible to all but a few playgoers. The *Chin-chui* was subjected to a thorough reappraisal, and modernized versions were performed in competition in Peking in June and July of 1964. The basic form was retained in the modernization but erotic and esoteric themes were no longer included. Although the reform movement has faced resistance by conservatives, the

34

new versions achieved immediate success. The influence of the
success was soon felt in Shanghai and throughout the country.

This movement of bringing the theater back to the people became
the foundation of the endeavors of the Great Cultural Revolution
in the field of the dramatic arts. As with ancient Greek drama,
Chinese classical plays are preserved in theory but performances
of *Chin-chui* are now limited to modernized versions. Although it
may seem strange to those accustomed to the traditional form of this
drama to see modern soldiers dancing with guns in their hands and
straw sandals on their feet, to the young Chinese, these modern
innovations blend easily with the old style and music of *Chin-chui*.

In China, entertainment also embraces an educational objective;
thus the life of the people finds expression in the mood and thought
of the Revolution, and life in Peking, unfettered by strict regulation
goes on in a relaxed way.

Low prices in Peking are not limited to foodstuffs, for other daily
necessities are also cheap—and plentiful. The city's shopping
centers and department stores are crowded from morning—when
many people wait outside for the stores to open—until evening.
This is partly accounted for by the fact that many of the factories
have two or three work shifts. Evenings and weekends are the most
crowded times, however. Since there are many nurseries in Peking,
a striking feature is the relatively small number of children seen
shopping with their parents, especially during weekdays.

Domestic goods of all kinds are sold, from nail clippers to
instant coffee (from Hainan Island). Sold in individual packets
for about two cents, the instant coffee is a standard item. Vegetables,

fruit, spices, foodstuffs, and daily necessities are sold in large quantities.

The central shopping area of Peking continues to be Wang Fu-ching, now called People's Road. Found here are department stores, a variety of food and clothing stores, and the main store of the New China Bookstore. On the street behind People's Road is the large Eastern Peace Market, renamed the Eastern Wind Market under the Great Cultural Revolution. Over six hundred shops, always crowded with customers, are crammed side by side in this market, which originated in 1903 as a collection of street stalls concentrated outside Tung-hua Gate. Although these shops were known in the past to overcharge and sometimes cheat customers, the market is operated on an honest basis under the present government.

An even larger market than Eastern Wind is the Hsi-tan Market. Established in 1932, it houses some 656 shops and serves the people on the west side of the city, although it is located not too far from its competitor. These two markets, together with the Tung-tan People's Market, established in 1951 near Lung-fu Temple, comprise the three markets of Peking.

When I first went to China, I hoped to stay there for one year, but had no idea whether permission would be forthcoming. Normal relations had not yet been restored between our two countries, and though non-governmental goodwill missions were a frequent occurrence, most of them stayed no more than a month or so. In principle, a Japanese was not permitted to stay in China for a long period. I was able to stay for over two years, probably because I was a historical research worker with no direct connection with politics.

The two subjects on which I hoped to do research were the ideas of Sun Yat-sen and the history of Sino-Japanese relations with particular reference to the South Manchurian Railway Company. It was arranged therefore that the Institute of Modern History of the Chinese Academy of Science should look after me, and a study room was provided for me within the Institute. My two years were spent doing research at the Institute, with trips to the provinces whenever my work so required.

The Institute of Modern History has 120 members researching in five fields—Chinese modern history, the history of imperialist incursions in China, the history of modern thought, the history of the labor movement, and the history of the Revolution (since the May Fourth Movement of 1919). The Institute is also a center for the assembly and collation of historical source materials. It is housed in a large, Chinese-style building in quiet surroundings, and has the kind of intellectual atmosphere common to such institutions in every country.

Research workers are given special consideration, and are not tied to strict working hours as are employees of ordinary enterprises. Being free to work at home, their lives are similar in many ways to those of scholars in Japan.

The remarkable development of the economy in many fields besides that of food-stuffs was apparent to the most casual observer during the two years I was there. The number of neon signs outside the shops increased, as did the number of cars on the streets, and living standards in general would seem to have risen at a considerable rate during the past two or three years.

Compared with the old semicolonial days, when famine was an annual occurrence in one or another part of the country and many

PEKING 火

beggars were to be seen in the streets, life in China today, when
death through starvation and beggars are equally unknown, has
a new stability which in itself is quite enough to make the ordinary
citizen sing the praises of the present. Nothing could be more
natural than the respect and affection the masses feel for Mao Tse-
tung whose political leadership has brought about such a state of
affairs.

Observers in the West marvel at the way the Chinese—intellectuals and peasants, old and young alike—go beyond this natural
feeling of affection for Mao and study his ideas avidly as though
they were a kind of magic wand that could make all difficulties
disappear. In Japan too, considerable mirth has been provoked by
stories such as that of the greengrocer whose watermelons sold
well as a result of his perusal of Mao's works.

However, in terms of the actualities of present-day China, there
is nothing odd in such stories. For the peasants and shop assistants
who first learned to read after the Revolution, the *Selected Works
of Mao Tse-tung* is the first real book they have ever possessed.
The book provides some reasonable solution, at least, to the
problems they face at the moment. The reader uses it to give him
some hint as to how to set about considering why, say, his watermelons do not sell. If no answer is forthcoming, he goes back to
Mao Tse-tung again; this intellectual shuttling to and fro is referred
to in China as "flexing the brain." By such means modern, rational
thought processes are automatically set in motion. In Japan, a
merchant whose watermelons did not sell would consult a textbook
on management and study market research and commodity control,
but in China no appropriate science of socialistic management has
yet emerged. The people, in short, with the aid of the works of

Mao, have begun to realize the need to think rationally and to replace the old with the new.

That a large section of the public should have begun to acquire logical ways of thinking must be accounted an important happening in a nation of some 700 million people which has hitherto always been so backward. It is this new force which China is making conscious use of in its Third Five-Year Plan.

Granted that the economy is on the road to prosperity, various contradictions still lurk just beneath the surface. One which I was frequently brought up against was the organization of the sales sections of commercial institutions. When one buys something at a department store, for example, a bill in triplicate has to be made out with carbon papers for even the most trifling purchase. The customer takes two copies to a cash desk in another part of the shop, where he pays. The woman at the desk keeps one copy of the bill and stamps and returns the other. The customer takes it back to the counter and gets his purchase in exchange. As I have already said, the mass-supply, mass-demand phenomenon is already apparent in China, and customers have to wait in line before the cash desk—so that a certain tension is naturally generated between customer and shop assistant.

I once asked a Chinese in a responsible position in the field of commerce why there were no self-service supermarkets in China. Nothing should be easier, I said, since shoplifters were unknown in China. In China, vegetables and fruit at the height of the season are piled up on the sidewalks, where they are left at night even after the shops have shut. So high is the standard of public morality that nothing is ever taken.

PEKING 北京

The reply to my query was that although there was no moral problem the supermarket, unfortunately, was impracticable in China. He gave two reasons.

First, he said, the living standard of the masses was still low and families bought only the precise amount, of say, soy sauce or oil that they needed at the time; so far there was no general habit of laying in a stock of any particular commodity. Secondly, the development of industry was still not uniform, and industrial production of the vinyl that would be necessary for wrapping up goods in fixed quantities was still insufficiently developed.

China still has all kinds of contradictions of this kind, resulting from the uneven rate of development of different sectors of the economy. Its leaders, however, apparently feel that such contradictions are a good thing; that, provided a decent solution is forthcoming, there is nothing better for stimulating social development.

Peking is officially known as the "Special City of Peking," and together with Shanghai comes under the direct control of the central government. It does not fall under the administrative control of Hopei Province, in which it is located. The provincial administration of Hopei Province is located now in Shih-chia Chuang.

Since the founding of the People's Republic of China, the old city of Peking has undergone great change. First, the old wall surrounding the Imperial City was gradually torn down and new buildings were put up, extending beyond the bounds of the old wall towards the outlying areas. The areas under direct municipal control expanded rapidly as the city's economy developed, though everything was based, of course, on proper town planning. At present, Peking comprises eight wards and nine districts. The suburban districts are, needless to say, mostly farming villages that have been organized as people's communes. Peking's ward administration scheme is as follows. The wards are Tung-ch'eng, Hsi-ch'eng, Ch'ung-wen, Hsüan-wu, (all of which are more or less within the old Imperial City), Ch'ao-yang, Feng-t'ai, Hai-tien, and Men-t'ou-kou. The districts are Ch'ang-p'ing, T'ung, Shun-i, Ta-hsing, Fang-shan, P'ing-ku, Huai-jou, Mi-yün, and Yen-ch'ing. The city encompasses an area of four thousand square miles and a population of over six million.

Although development in the outlying districts of Peking is surprising, the greatest changing influence on the city's appearance has been the extension of its streets immediately outside the old city wall. Where once farming villages were a step outside the wall, the urban streets have now burst their bonds and are spreading to the north, west, and east.

On the west side of the old city, an area extending about two-thirds of a mile out from the old Fu-hsing Gate has become a new extension of Hsi-ch'ang Street and is used primarily for government offices. To the north, government offices extend in an area of approximately the same width. Beyond I-ho Park, to the northwest, there is an area comprising many educational institutions.

To the north of the old city wall, the northern outlying districts between An-ting Gate and Te-sheng Gate are being developed as a new housing area to adjoin the educational district in the northwest.

Since the Great Leap Forward of 1958, construction of a large group of housing estates in this area, centering around Ho-p'ing-li, has gone ahead and today the area is still being enlarged in scope. The Ho-p'ing-li housing development contains primary and middle schools, nurseries, hotels, and other facilities, and there are more than one hundred apartment buildings of four or five floors each. In addition, there are many groupings of independent houses in the northern suburbs, with parks (including the Young People's Park), theaters and leisure centers in between. All these are supplied with gas and water. Compared with the older parts of the city, where the existence of old stone paving has hindered the development toward modern structures and facilities, this new area of the city is a harbinger of what is to come in Peking's future.

Thus in the area embracing educational districts of the northwest suburbs and the new housing area of the northern suburbs, one can see the results of city planning providing for huge multi-story buildings, but in the neighboring suburbs the demeanor of the land is still a rustic one, with only occasional factories or government offices.

Proceeding further south, that is, on the east side of the Tung-chih Gate and Ch'ao-yang Gate, the cultural area centering around the Workers' Gymnasium and Stadium and the Agricultural Exhibit Hall is located. Still further south, in the area outside Chien-kuo Gate, the area opposite Fu-hsing Gate on the west side is balanced by more public government offices and apartment buildings for those who work there. Most of the foreign embassies that were previously located along Tung-chiao-min-hsiang (now called Anti-Imperialist Road) in the old city have moved to this location.

Plans call for factories to be located around the east and south suburbs, but the southern suburbs still have a predominantly rural aspect. There are a number of important plant areas around the city, such as the plant at Shih-ching Hill in the western suburbs and the car plant at Ch'ang-hsin-tien in the southwestern suburbs, which provide focal points for their immediate localities.

In feudal times Peking was not only already the political heart of China but the center of a consumer culture as well. The time when life in the city flourished at its highest point was precisely that when its character as a consumption center was most clear. According to Marxist theory (Capital Vol. III), the prosperity of Asian cities, or more precisely the existence of Asian cities, is closely connected to government expenditures. Peking has become a model illustration of what Marx said about Asian cities. From the beginning of China's semi-feudal, semi-colonial period, a number of ne style factories were built, but they were restricted to production of consumer goods. Peking was under the control of imperialists and the bureaucratic-capitalist control of mine owners, companies, and banks. This has all changed now, and with the development of the people's economy motive power, fuel, machinery, building materials, chemicals, spinning, and other industries have got under way. These and other new industries are approaching the international level. Peking is being transformed into a productive rather than a consumption center, with the foundations for a modern industry already more or less completed.

Prior to the PLA victory in China, Ch'ing-hua and Yen-ching universities were located in the northwestern suburbs of Peking. The predecessor of Ch'ing-hua University, Ch'ing-hua School was a school to prepare students for study in America, founded in 1911, using "reparation" money from the Boxer uprising which

PEKING 火

was returned to the Ch'ing dynasty government by America on condition that it be used for cultural education. After the school came under the control of the Republican government it was made into a national university, but because of its provenance the "Ching-hua spirit" meant a kind of elite outlook derived from its concentration on future study in America. Yen-ching University was an American-style school closely associated with Harvard University, and its dean until 1949 was an American named Stewart. On August 18, 1949, Mao Tse-tung wrote to the dean: "Good-bye Stewart."

Most other schools, including the national Peking University and many other official and private universities were located in the old Imperial City. Peking University was first established in 1898, toward the end of the Ch'ing dynasty, as the Ching-shih Institute. Its Red Tower at Sha-tung rose above the old city as a symbol of its authority as China's leading educational institution.

These universities have a colorful history of student movements such as the May 4 Movement and the December 9 Movement. However, since in the old China the only students who could go on to university belonged to the privileged classes, they were naturally prey to an elite consciousness and an over-preoccupation with advancement in life.

With the new government, however, a move began to reorganize universities and colleges, and at the same time to refashion the outlook of the intellectuals, thus starting a new era in Chinese university education. Ch'ing-hua University had its humanities departments moved to Peking University and it became a comprehensive industrial university. Yen-ching University was done away with and Peking University moved onto its spacious campus. Construction of the educational area in the northwestern suburbs began; in the area of Ch'ing-hua University "Academy Road" was built, and most institutes of higher education as well as various research institutes, were concentrated here. Peking University and People's University, together with the Peking Aviation Institute, the Petroleum Institute, and many other colleges were established in the area. In addition, the Central Institute of the Races was set up to train the leaders of China's racial minorities. The Institute of Socialism, a research institute for members of the democratic parties, and the Institute of Agricultural Science are also in this area.

Not only university students, but high school students, Pioneers, and even the children in nurseries, are all being trained as successors of the revolution, a policy that is being consistently carried out in China today. This task of training successors of the revolution —known in Chinese as *chieh-pan jen*—so that there will be no reversion to capitalism is considered one of the most important undertakings in their society.

To train these children and young people means to hand over to them the traditions of the revolution. In order to pass on the revolutionary traditions of the previous generation, the successors listen to the personal experiences of their predecessors, consider them, and learn from them. It is the business of the predecessors to "pass on" the traditions, and this must be done well if youth is to learn well. The combination of "teaching" and "learning" is the work of "fixing" the revolution as a common experience in the minds of the people. Here, it is believed, lies the key to creating the future.

To this end, a constant emphasis in instruction in the schools, in the training of the Pioneers, and in movies and plays in general is to ensure that easier times will never make people forget the hardships of the past which, alone, have made today possible. A characteristic feature of Chinese politics is that the demand for motive power for progress is not sought in a vision of the good life of the future, but in the "memory of difficulties." This is obvious wherever one goes in Peking.

It was this concept of teaching about "past hardships" that led to the compilation of the "Four Histories of Peking" series, which deals with the histories of families, villages, factories and people's communes; moreover people are taught not only the history of their own country, but the "memories of hardship" of other peoples as well. The basis for this way of thinking is, of course, the *Thoughts of Mao Tse-tung*.

Peking, the city symbolized by the Gate of Heavenly Peace, also leads the nation in the study of Mao's philosophy, and its inhabitants seem to feel it their duty to serve as a kind of base for spreading the revolution throughout the nation. With its combination of tradition and creativity, the city is a source of great pride to its citizens—a pride that will doubtless ensure that the construction already begun will be continued in the future too. And it will be the *chieh-pan jen* who will take the lead in it, for Peking today is a city of youth. Since this is so, it seems fitting to conclude with a passage from the *Thoughts of Mao Tse-tung* addressed specifically to the nation's youth:

"The world is yours, as well as ours, but in the last analysis, it is yours. You young people, full of vigor and vitality, are in the bloom of life, like the sun at eight or nine in the morning. Our hope is placed on you.

"The world belongs to you. China's future belongs to you."

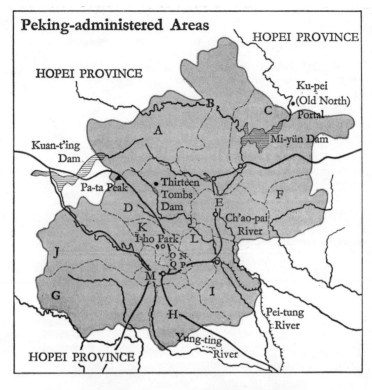

Peking-administered Areas

HOPEI PROVINCE

HOPEI PROVINCE

Ku-pei
(Old North)
Portal

Kuan-t'ing
Dam

Mi-yün Dam

Pa-ta Peak

Thirteen
Tombs
Dam

Ch'ao-pai
River

I-ho Park

Pei-tung
River

HOPEI PROVINCE

Yung-ting
River

A	Yen-ch'ing District	J	Men-t'ou-kou Ward
B	Huai-jou District	K	Hai-tien Ward
C	Mi-yün District	L	Ch'ao Yang Ward
D	Ch'ang-p'ing District	M	Feng-t'ai Ward
E	Shun-i District	N	Tung-ch'eng Ward
F	P'ing-ku District	O	Hsi-ch'eng Ward
G	Fang-shan District	P	Ch'ung-wen Ward
H	Ta-hsing District	Q	Hsüan-wu Ward
I	T'ung District		

(*The last four wards form central Peking and its immediate environs.*)

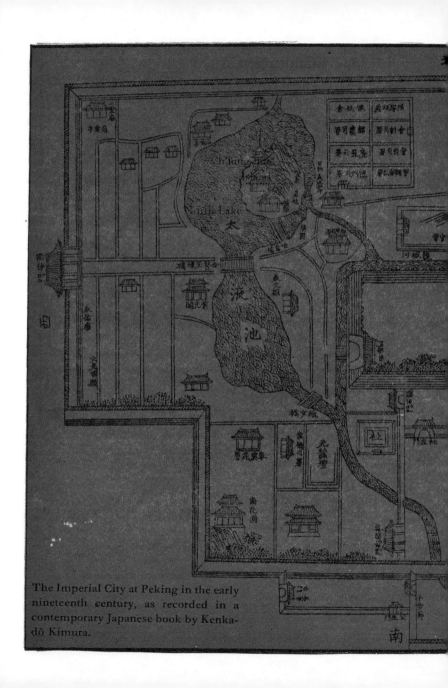

The Imperial City at Peking in the early nineteenth century, as recorded in a contemporary Japanese book by Kenkadō Kimura.

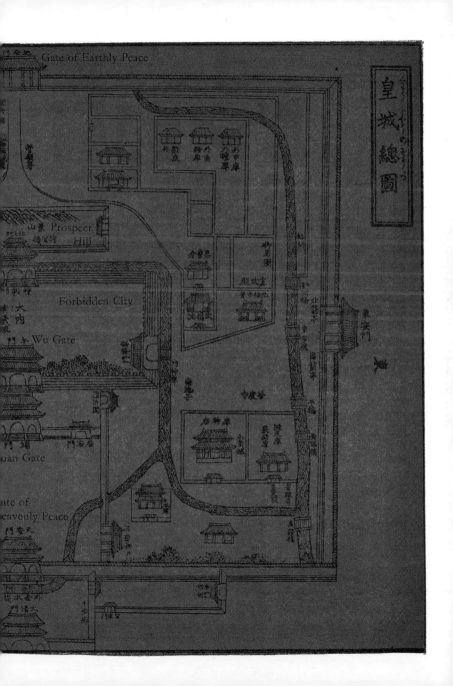

Gate of Earthly Peace

皇城總圖

外庫

外御庫

Prospect
Hill

Forbidden City

大内

Wu Gate

東安門

uan Gate

ate of

eavenly Peace

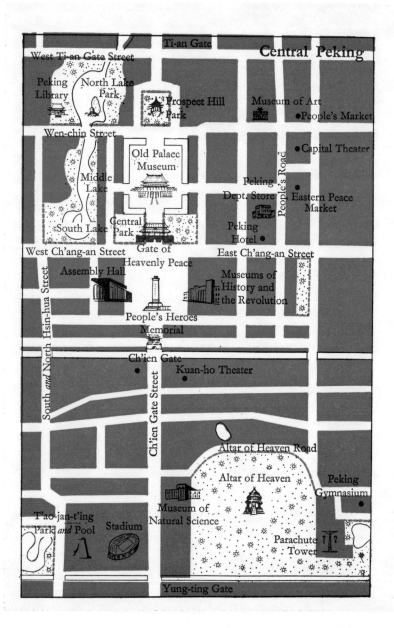

Chronology of Peking

B.C.

1200 Sedentary culture of Yin flourishes on lower reaches of Yellow River

1100 King Wu of Chou kills king of Yin and occupies central plain

1000 Chi Ch'eng (ancient Peking) develops as a feudal state situated just west of Kuang-an Gate in present-day Peking

222 Feudal state of Ch'in becomes dominant and makes Chi Ch'eng stronger as political, military, and economic center; Chi Ch'eng becomes most vital northeast border defense point until end of T'ang

221 First emperor of Ch'in unifies country and begins construction of the Great Wall as protection against the Hsiung-nu (Huns)

202 Han (Former Han) dynasty established

A.D.

229 Period of Three Kingdoms begins

304 Period of Five Barbarian States and Sixteen Kingdoms begins

589 China unified under the Sui dynasty

618 T'ang dynasty established; Min-chung (present Fa-yuan) Temple built to honor battle-dead of Emperor T'ai-tsung; Chi Ch'eng enlarged about 3,410 yards east and west and 4,380 yards north and south

907 Period of Five Dynasties and Sixteen States

916 King of Khitan Tartars becomes emperor; dynasty later called Liao

938 Peking is called Nanking by Liao

960 Sung dynasty established

1115 Liao overcome by Yuchen Tartars; Chin dynasty established

1153 King Hai-ling of Chin moves his capital to Peking and enlarges Chung-tu (imperial palace)

1179 Shih-tsung builds detached palace at North Lake and constructs Ch'iung-hua Island

1189 Construction of Lu-kou Bridge begins (completed in 1192)

1215 Mongols destroy Chung-tu

1264 Kublai Khan moves his capital to Peking and calls it Ta-tu
1267 New area adjacent to northeast Chung-tu established
1275 Marco Polo visits Ta-tu; praises its size and beauty
1368 Ming dynasty established
1403 Emperor Yung-le plans rebuilding of Peking and Old Palace
1420 Emperor Yung-le moves to Peking; calls it "Northern Capital"
to differentiate it from the "Southern Capital" (Nanking)
1552 Japanese pirates attack Chekiang Province; outer palace built for
greater protection
1562 Russian envoy reaches Peking
1601 Matteo Ricci builds church in Peking
1629 Troops of the Latter Chin beseige Peking
1638 Troops of the Ch'ing (Manchu) attack Peking
1644 Li Tzu-ch'eng, leader of peasant army, takes Peking; Ming
emperor commits suicide and Ch'ing troops occupy city
1664 Dutch governor of Batavia sends mission to Peking
1669 Trade begins with Russia
1698 Forbidden City and T'ai-ho Hall constructed
1751 Envoy from Burma arrives in Peking
1753 Envoy from Siam arrives
1796 White Lotus uprising (continues to 1804)
1794 Mission sent from Holland
1813 T'ien-li Sect attacks Peking
1816 Lord Amherst, special envoy from Great Britain, arrives
1839 Opium War begins (continues to 1842)
1842 Treaty of Nanking, Hongkong ceded to Great Britain; beginning
of unequal treaties
1850 Taiping Rebellion (continues to 1862)
1860 British and French forces enter Peking and burn Yüan-ming;
Treaty of Peking signed in October
1861 Office of Prime Minister established
1893 Railroad between Peking and Shanghai opened
1894 Sino-Japanese War
1898 Ching-shih Institute (later Peking University) established
1900 Boxer uprising; troops of the Eight Powers land and Empress
Tz'u Hsi flees to Sian
1902 Empress Tz'u Hsi returns to Peking
1905 Treaty signed in Peking between China and Japan over Manchuria
1911 Wuchang insurrection

1912 Ch'ing dynasty ends; Yuan Shih-k'ai becomes President of Republic

1915 Japan presents 21 demands

1917 Literary revolution begins

1918 New parliament convenes in Peking in August; proposal to unify language. Li Ta-chao and others organize Marxist study group in Peking

1919 May Fourth Movement; Peking student group demonstrates against Japan

1920 First May Day celebrations held in China. Declaration of unity

1921 Chinese Communist Party founded in July. Excavation of Peking Man

1922 Soviet representative enters Peking

1924 Reorganization of political parties completed in January. Feng Yü-hsiang attempts coup in October. Sun Yat-sen enters Peking in December

1925 Sun Yat-sen dies in March in Peking

1926 May 18 Incident. Chang Tso-lin enters Peking in December. Chiang Kai-shek's troops move north in July

1927 Chang Tso-lin organizes military government in Peking in June

1928 Chiang Kai-shek's troops enter Peking in June; change its name to Peip'ing. Chang Tso-lin retreats and the north brought under government control. Chiang Kai-shek becomes head of the Republic

1930 Yen Hsi-shan sets up rebel government but suppressed with help of Chang Hsueh-liang. Name of capital changed back to Peking

1931 Manchurian Incident

1932 Shanghai Incident

1933 Japanese troops approach Peking

1934 Communist forces begin the Long March (continues into 1935)

1935 December 9 Movement. Peking students lead demonstration against Japanese puppet government in the north

1936 Ch'ao-yang Gate Incident. Chinese Communists call for resistance against Japanese in March. Lu Hsün dies in October. Sian Incident in December

1937 Incident at Marco Polo Bridge (Lu-kou) in July. Provisional Chinese government formed in Peking in December

1942 Yenan reform movement initiated

1945 Japan surrenders. Soviet-Chinese treaty signed. Chiang and Mao agree to meet in October

1946 Chiang and Mao meet in Chungking. Civil war intensifies from August

1948 U.S. signs economic aid agreement in June

1949 Chinese Liberation Army enters Peking in January. General offensive begins on the Yangtze front in April. People's Republic of China founded in October

1950 Chinese-Soviet Treaty of Friendship signed

1952 San-fan Wu-fan Movement. Asian-Pacific Area Peace Conference

1953 First Five-year Plan begins

1956 "Hundred Flowers" movement begins. Eighth plenary party assembly in September

1957 Anti-Rightist Campaign begins

1958 National Structural Reform and Second Five-year Plan decided on. Commune system initiated

1959 Natural disasters begin (continue to 1962). Three-stage system in commune structure started to correct the economy

1960 Soviets cut off economic aid to China

1963 Socialist Education Campaign among farmers begins. July conference between Chinese and Soviet leaders

1964 Soviet-Chinese quarrel intensifies. China explodes first nuclear device

1965 Yao Wen-yüang's criticism of Wu Han (Deputy Mayor of Peking) heralds the beginning of the Great Proletarian Cultural Revolution

1966 Cultural Revolution begins in April; Peng Chen purged in June. Eleventh plenary session of Central Committee opens in August and Cultural Revolution becomes official. Eleventh anniversary of the People's Republic celebrated by 1,500,000 in Peking, focusing around the Red Guard

1967 Struggle for control in Shanghai. Great Cultural Revolution enters new stage. Peking Municipal Revolutionary Committee Formed

4. *Wall of Nine Dragons* (Chi-lung Pi) in the center of North Lake (Pei Hai) Park. Built during the Mongol rule of the Yüan dynasty, the wall·is eighty-eight feet long. Each side is decorated with nine dragons. There is also a Wall of Nine Dragons in the Old Palace.

55

5. *View of the Old Palace* and Peking from Prospect Hill (Ching Shan). Converted into a public park, Prospect Hill lies just north of the former Forbidden City and provides a fine vantage point for viewing Peking. In the foreground is Shen-wu (Spirit of Bravery) Gate, now plastered with revolutionary posters, and behind it the yellow roofs of the Old Palace buildings. The Gate of Heavenly Peace is visible at the far end.

57

8. *Demonstration in support* of the ▶ Great Cultural Revolution (*see overleaf*) is accompanied by beating drums, wailing horns, and clanging cymbals in the bright April sunshine.

◀6. *View of rooftops* in a Peking residential area reveals the overall somber appearance given to the city by the standardized gray roofing tiles. Houses of two stories were forbidden in Peking by an old imperial edict, resulting in low, one-storied houses stretching from tiled roof to tiled roof.

7. *Back street* under the Great Cultural Revolution shows effects of the current struggle in China. A portrait of Mao Tse-tung hangs over the house entrance and the words of Mao adorn the wall. Although in earlier times it was customary for a single family to occupy one house, several families now generally live in the equivalent space.

9. *Ch'i-nien* (*Annual Prayer*) *Hall*, located at the Altar of Heaven, south of the Old Palace, once served as a place where the emperors offered prayers for rich harvests. About 124 feet high and almost one hundred feet in diameter, the building was constructed in the early fifteenth century by the Mings.

10. *T'ai-ho* (*Supreme Harmony*)▶ *Gate* in the old Forbidden City. This perfectly symmetrical structure was originally built in Ming times, but has been restored several times since. It is approached through the Wu (Noon) Gate and over the Bridge of Golden Water.

Revolution and renovation have wrought many changes in the old city of Peking. But its ancient civilization, symbolized by the Great Wall of China to the north, continues to live on in the form of the many historical sites and structures that have been preserved to the present. Although the traditional culture is being re-evaluated and changed to suit the temper of modern China, it is not being destroyed. Indeed, it has permeated the hearts of the people and is reflected in their lives.

It is surprising how historical things are kept alive and closely associated with daily life. The Marco Polo Bridge, for example, where the Sino-Japanese war of 1937 started, is still in use today. It was built centuries ago, to span the Yung-ting River during the Ch'ien-lung era of the Ch'ing dynasty. The garden of the old emperors at North Lake has been converted into a public park. The traditional legacy of Peking is deeply rooted in the hearts of the people—and gives the city its charm.

Old Palace

11. *Wu* (*Noon*) *Gate*, the huge main entrance to the old Forbidden City, now guards the Old Palace Museum.

◀12. *T'ai-ho* (*Supreme Harmony*) *Hall*, facing a large courtyard of paved stones, once served as the stage for imperial ceremonies.

13. *Bridge of Golden Water* (Chinshi Ch'iao), just inside▶ Wu Gate, spans a small moat. The bridge is constructed of beautiful marble.

14. *Pavilion of Ten Thousand Springs* (Wan-ch'un T'ing), one of several structures that add architectural grace to the old Imperial Garden, once served as a resthouse for imperial consorts.

Gate of Heavenly Peace

15. *Gate of Heavenly Peace* (T'ien-an Men), symbol of the revolution and the site from which Mao Tsetung proclaimed the People's Republic of China, is the main entrance to the old Imperial City.

16. *Marble pillar* symbolizing heavenly peace is topped by a figure of a mythological lion and engraved with motifs of dragons and stylized clouds. Behind the pillar are observation stands.

17. *People's Assembly Hall*, the Chinese equivalent of the Capitol, stands on the west side of the square in front of the Gate of Heavenly Peace. Its great hall will hold ten thousand people and its banquet hall has a capacity of five thousand.

18. *Memorial to the People's Heroes* is engraved with a quote from Mao Tse-tung that reads "The People's Heroes Will Be Remembered Eternally." Around the base are relief carvings depicting historical events dating from the Opium War of the mid-nineteenth century.

19. *Portrait of Wu Tse-t'ien* in the Museum of History. Painted in fine detail, the subject was a powerful ruler during the early T'ang dynasty.

20. *Porcelain of fine design* and exquisite finish dating from the Ch'ien-lung era of the Ch'ing dynasty. On display in the Old Palace Museum, these pieces reflect the full maturity of Chinese culture of the period.

21. *Bronze vessel of the Yin* period on display with other works of art in the Museum of History. This heavy, imposing work from China's misty past speaks eloquently of the greatness of her ancient civilization.

22. *Historical Museum of the Revolution* stands across the square from the People's Assembly Hall, which it rivals in size. Historical items from the Opium wars through the communist revolution are on display. Children can often be found at play on the plaza.

23. *North Lake (Pei Hai) Park* built around the northernmost of three artificial lakes within the old Imperial City. This and the parks around the other lakes were once strictly for imperial use, but North Lake is now open to the public. It has been renamed "Park of Workers, Farmers, and Soldiers."

24. *A smiling girl* poses for a photograph in front of the Wall of Nine Dragons, one of the many famous sights in North Lake Park. On holidays, people flock to this park, a mecca for photographers. A large number of professional photographers also offer their services to tourists.

25. *Children's playground* in North Lake Park is a favorite of parents as well as children. Such playgrounds are appropriate in a country that loves the young.

26. *Rowboats on the lake* in North Lake Park, a popular place for families and lovers. When people tire of strolling in the park, they often rent rowboats and relax on the lake. An entrance pass for one year costs less than one dollar, with free access given to all on official holidays.

27. *Nan-ta Gate, entrance to the Altar of Heaven Park,* where the emperors once passed to pay homage to heaven, today displays quotations from Mao Tse-tung. The facade of the temple can be seen through the portal.

28. *Hall of Annual Prayer,* the central structure in the Altar of Heaven Park, stands on a three-tiered terrace. One of Peking's finest works of architecture, it was used by the emperors when offering prayers for rich harvests.

29. *Altar of Heaven* (T'ien-t'an), aligned on
a north-south axis, includes the Yüan-ch'iu
(*foreground*), a marble terrace, the Huang-
ch'iung Yü, a single-roofed hall, and the
Ch'i-nien Tien (Hall of Annual Prayer).

30. *Huang-Ch'iung Yü* was originally an
altar for offerings to heaven by the emperors.

31. *Panoramic view of I-ho Park*, in the northwest suburbs of Peking, from the Temple of Everlasting Longevity. Construction was begun on this extensive park as the site of a detached palace during the Yüan dynasty, but it was completed much later. The park includes the famous Temple of Everlasting Longevity (Wan-shou Szu) and K'un-ming Lake. In the background can be seen Shih-ch'i-k'ung Bridge and Yueh-po Tower.

81

32. *Entrance to I-ho Park*, which has been renamed "People's Park," carries slogans in support of the Great Proletarian Cultural Revolution. City buses, and tourist buses on holidays, provide transportation to the park from central Peking.

33. *Triumphal Arch* at the Pavilion of the ▶ Fragrant Buddha atop Wan-shou (Everlasting Longevity) Hill. Situated below the pavilion, which affords a view of distant Peking, the arch opens out onto K'un-ming Lake. Shih-ch'i-k'ung Bridge and Yueh-po Tower can be seen off to the left.

34. *Stone boat in I-ho Park's K'un-ming Lake* ▶ (*see overleaf*) serves as a reminder of China's past glories to the many sightseers. Constructed entirely of stone for the pleasure of Empress Hsi-t'ai, the "boat" has facilities for serving refreshments.

35–6. *Long Corridor (left) and the Tower of Many Treasures (above)*. Long corridors similar to this connect the numerous buildings at K'un-ming Lake. This one is 2,366 feet long; long enough, it is said, for the first words of love to be spoken at one end and marriage decided at the other.

87

37. *T'ien-ning Szu* (*above*) a temple situated slightly west of the boundary between the former Imperial City and the Forbidden City, has more than two thousand figures of Buddha carved in its walls.

38. *Temple of True Remembrance* (Chen-chueh Szu), situated north of Peking Zoo, was built during Ming times in imitation of Indian architecture. Forces of the Eight Powers looted many of its treasures.

39. *Temple of the White Pagoda* (Pai-t'a Szu), in the residential part of western Peking, dates from the Liao dynasty but has been rebuilt often. Echoing the Lamaistic style, it long ago lost its religious significance and no longer functions as a temple.

40. *Pavilion of Bountiful Fortune* (Wan-fu Ko), situated within the palace grounds, forms part of the huge Lama Temple of Peking. Many unusual Buddhist paintings and sculptures are found here, including a great statue of Buddha some 104 feet high in the main temple.

41. *Leng-en Hall*: modeled after T'ai-ho Hall, and located at the foot of T'ien-shou Hill, the site of the Thirteen Tombs of Ming, the building is unusual in China for its

wooden construction. These huge tombs for the emperors of the Ming dynasty have underground chambers that are said to still contain many treasures.

42. *Triumph Arch*
(*above*) at the Thir-
teen Tombs of
Ming opens onto
an asphalt walk
that is lined on
both sides with
stone statues of
various animals,
some twenty-four
in all. The arch
itself is richly deco-
rated.

美援抗越

43. *Ceiling in the Leng-en Hall* presents a colorful pattern of great beauty. The ceiling is some thirty-five feet high and is supported by a pillar so huge that two adults cannot touch fingertips when embracing it.

44. *Ming Tower at the Tombs* houses a stone tablet dedicated to the first Ming emperor. Behind the tower is an earthen mound thought to cover an ancient palace; it is yet to be excavated. The revolutionary slogan calls for support of the North Vietnamese.

45–8. *Stone sculptures at the Thirteen Tombs of Ming.* The figures of animals here are usually in pairs, with the female of each species seated and the male standing. A Red Guard pamphlet has been pasted on the trunk of the elephant statue shown on the left. The figure of a ferocious guardian warrior sculpted in the battle dress of the Mings is shown at upper left; at upper right is the figure of a minister of state affairs in formal attire. To the right is a stone image of a mythical animal said capable of distinguishing the bad from the good.

49. *Chu-yung Barrier Gate,* the closest in the Great Wall to Peking, was the capital's ancient portal to the western lands. Built in 1343, during the Yüan dynasty, it was also the gate for cultural influences from the West.

50. *View of Chu-yung Barrier Gate,* built between the two mountains. The railway seen beyond the gate connects Peking and Chang-chia K'ou. It was the first to be planned and built by Chinese without foreign assistance. Now bypassed by a modern road, the gate has fallen into disuse.

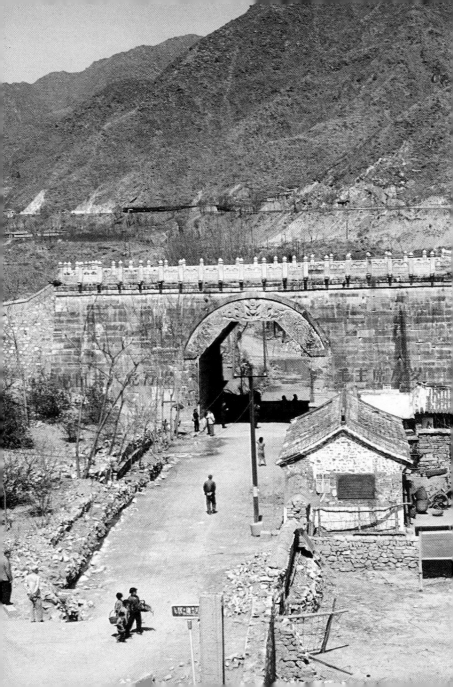

51. *The Great Wall of China*, timeless symbol of China's ancient history. Construction started on the wall some 2,500 years ago, during the Chou dynasty. Enlarged in the Ch'in dynasty, it extends some 3,400 miles.

Nurtured by its old tradition, Peking is a sedate and peaceful city. This feeling is even manifested in the way its people walk. They do not have the jouncing walk of the Cantonese, nor do they have the busy walk of Tokyoites. The way they walk may be described as truly placid and deliberate. When combined with the vigor of the Great Cultural Revolution, with its loud, chanted slogans accompanied by drums and gongs, it is quite interesting and almost humorous. The tradition of napping after lunch is also kept alive, as are many of the old customs of daily life.

People's Communes

52. *Children of the People's Commune of Chinese-Albanian Amity*. In the suburbs of Peking, this commune produces vegetables for the city. After three years of natural calamities, the commune is slowly developing.

53–4. *Interior views of the commune living quarters*. Although poor compared with city homes, these quarters contain items—a radio, a doll case, a clock, and a thermos bottle—that were beyond the dreams of farmers of old. The traditional picture of the God of Wealth has been replaced by the omnipresent portrait of Mao.

55–6. *Rural scenes on the outskirts of* ▶ *Peking*. Organized into communes, farms in the area produce vegetables and dairy products for Peking. Farmers here lead an easier life than those in more distant communes. Tree-lined rural roads (*see overleaf*), with trees sometimes two or three rows deep, are one of the many surprising aspects of China.

57–9. *Facets of farm life* on one of the many communes around Peking show unusual techniques for raising hogs and cattle. The easy-to-clean, sanitary pens, permitting more efficient fattening, are a source of pride to these farmers.

60. *Ducks on a commune pond* (*see* ▶ *overleaf*) swim, blissfully unaware they may be scheduled for the table as the famous Peking roast duck. Raised on a mass-production basis because of the great demand, these ducks are force fed.

61–2. *Transplanting rice and cutting hay* on the People's Commune of the Red Star. "Ships in the south, horses in the north," runs an old Chinese saying. Once wheat was the main crop of North China, with little rice

grown save for the imperial offerings to heaven. But today the land is crisscrossed by irrigation ditches. Planting and harvesting scenes such as the ones pictured here are common.

63. *View of the Drum Tower* (Ku Lou) from Prospect Hill, looking north, away from the Gate of Heavenly Peace. In the foreground is the Culture Palace for Youth and on both sides of the street next to it are the blue-green roofs of dormitories built by the present government. Beyond the distant Drum Tower is the Bell Tower (Chung Lou).

65. *Drum Tower and its surroundings,* once an area of shops. Today the Drum Tower is used as a cultural club building and is plastered with pamphlets of the Great Cultural Revolution. The bus is taking participants to a demonstration. Peking's buses are painted red, its trolleys are blue.

64. *Ch'ang-an (Lasting Peace) Street* during morning commuting time. Workers off to their jobs make good use of bicycles, the main form of private transportation in China. There are an estimated five million bicycles in Peking. Unlike the nerve-racking, taxi-crowded streets of Tokyo and New York, those of Peking are often filled only with bicycles.

66. *Main store of the New China Bookshop* on People's Road (formerly Wang Fu-ching). "Big character" newspapers cover the windows and a portrait of Mao hangs over the entrance.

67. *Eastern Wind Market*, next to the New China Bookstore, acquired its present name during the Great Cultural Revolution. It was formerly called the Eastern Peace Market. With a sixty-year tradition, the market contains six hundred stalls.

68. *Peking's main street* east of the Morning Sun (Ch'ao-yang) Gate leads from the Old Palace to the suburbs. Although this street is serviced by trolleys, bicycles still comprise its main form of traffic.

115

69. *Bell Tower (Chung Lou)*, north of the Drum Tower, stands on the north side of the wide street leading from the Gate of Earthly Peace. Built in the era of Emperor Yung-le, the stone tower long housed a great bell that tolled the time. Today the bell lies on the ground north of the Drum Tower, a relic of the past.

70. *Museum of Chinese Art* at the eastern
end of People's Road is noted for its
traditional architectural style. A wide range
of Chinese works of art are on display at all
times here. The portrait of Mao Tse-tung
and the white-on-red slogans of the Great
Cultural Revolution are familiar sights.

117

71. *Agricultural Exhibit Hall* in the eastern suburbs is famous for its displays of model farms, new agricultural implements, and other exhibits. It is the largest institution built in Peking since 1949, covering over 160,000 square feet of area. Farmers from all over China visit the institution.

72. *Peking Workers' Stadium*, near the Peking Gymnasium, seats eighty thousand people. Peking's pride, it contains facilities for lodging fifteen hundred athletes as well as a cafeteria and movie theater.

73. *Peking Station*, built during the Great Leap Forward of 1958, is the same size as Tokyo Station. In addition to international trains servicing Hanoi, Moscow, and Ulan Bator, there are five domestic lines.

74. *Subway construction site* shows progress on a line that will eventually connect Peking Station and Shih-ching Hill. This subway plan is the first step in a scheme that will see subways throughout the city.

75. *Cultural Palace of the Races*, a combination club and hotel used by the racial minorities of China when they visit Peking. This beautiful building, with its blue-green tile roofs, is located on West Ch'ang-an Street. It contains displays showing the actual conditions of the racial minorities in China.

76–7. *Racial minority groups* participating in the celebration of a national holiday. China's racial minority population is about thirty-eight million, most living in border areas. Shown here are members of the I tribe, in high leather boots, and the Miao tribe.

78. *Costumes* of a number of minority groups: the long skirts of Koreans, the open sleeves of Tibetans, the black blouses of Miao, and the small hats of the European-looking Uighurs.

123

Shih-san Ling (Thirteen Hills) Dam

79. *Observation platform* atop Shih-san Ling Dam provides a point of color for this huge structure. Located in the suburbs of Peking, this is one of several large dams that supply the city with drinking water and the farms with irrigation water.

80. *Shih-san Ling Dam* is located behind the Thirteen Tombs of Ming and was completed in May, 1958. Although not particularly large, it is famous because Mao Tse-tung and other high officials participated directly in its construction by carrying building materials. It is about twenty times the size of K'un-ming Lake.

81.   *Kuan-t'ing* (*National*) *Dam* viewed from Pa-ta Peak. The dam is barely visible off to the left. Located to the northwest of Peking, it and Mi-yun Dam are among the largest in China.

82.   *Side street scene* ▶ (*see overleaf*) shows the typical Peking residential community of old earthwork houses and stone pavements. Down such streets and off the main thoroughfares are found the ordinary people, who keep alive the old spirit of Peking. The Great Cultural Revolution has seeped into these back streets, however, and slogans as well as the words of Mao adorn the walls of houses.

83. *Modern apartment buildings* in the suburbs: the new face of a changing China. Such
apartment complexes are spreading rapidly,
a contrast with the unchanging life of those
living in the old city.

84–5. *Street-cleaning scenes* (*see overleaf*) ▶
reflect new responsibilities in China. Each
block is organized into a Neighborhood Committee. In the bottom picture, soldiers take
a break from their cleaning duties.

86. *Aerial view of Ch'ang-an Square (see preceding page, overleaf)* Although the city in general has become dirty under the stress of the Great Cultural Revolution, this square is an exception. People about their own business walk unconcernedly over slogans of the Great Cultural Revolution painted on the pavement.

87. *Delivery man* with a load of milk from a commune. Dairy products are popular and many communes raise milch cows to keep up with an increasing demand. Milk deliveries are made early in the morning; both large and small bottles are available.

88. *Bicycle parking lot* for some of Peking's five million bicycles. It costs slightly less than one cent to park a bicycle here for one day. Tokens made of bamboo are issued for identification.

133

Although the clothing of Chinese students is not of fine quality, it is always clean. So, too, are the parks and streets, which are looked after by the students as an extracurricular activity. Their education has been planned with an eye to the future: they will be the new leaders of this vast nation and their responsibilities will be many.

89. *Running drill* early in the morning is common—and often surprising to visitors. Students, work units, and individuals voluntarily run around the block as a form of morning exercise: one gets the impression that China is a country of runners.

90. *Group of young demonstrators* celebrating the establishment of the Peking Municipal Revolutionary Committee. These students, at a rest area, wear carefree expressions.

91. *Red Guard members* relax with a cup of tea in front of the Chinese Museum. They wear the insignia of their "struggle group."

92. *Bright-faced children* at a commune nursery participate in group activities. Each commune maintains a nursery, allowing parents to give their full attention to production. Communes in the suburbs of Peking are noted for their fine facilities.

93. *National Athletic Meet* at the Peking Workers' Stadium. Over three thousand athletes, including representatives from all parts of China, form complex Chinese characters over a period of seventy minutes. These mass games were held to acclaim the revolution.

94–5 *Curious citizens of Peking* (*see overleaf*) read "big character" newspapers. The top photo was taken at Peking University and the one at the bottom at the Central Institute of Races. The first "big character" newspapers were made and displayed at Peking University on June 1, 1966, by students and instructors under the leadership of Mao Tsetung. This famous event launched the Great Proletarian Cultural Revolution. The billboards in the bottom photo criticize government officials.

96. *Cyclists hurrying to join a demonstration* (*see overleaf, facing page*). A large drum is carried on the back of one bicycle. Demonstrations are noisy and colorful affairs, more like parades than political activism.

139

◄ 97. *Students of Peking University* at play. Despite constant political activities, students, the vanguard of the Great Cultural Revolution, take time for recreation.

98. *Young people boating at North Lake Park*. A great change took place in the lives of the Chinese people after the present government was proclaimed in 1949. It seems that all over China youth predominates. Left, bottom, young men are shown spending a free day boating.

99. *Boys and girls of a Pioneer group* taking part in a celebration. All children of seven become members of the Pioneers when they enter primary school.

◄ **100.** *Supporters of the Great Cultural Revolution* (*see preceding page*) hang signs and paint the words of Mao on walls. It is an old Chinese custom to hang signs with felicitous sayings over building entrances.

146

101. *Noisy demonstration* in support of the establishment of the Peking Municipal Revolutionary Committee. Workers, students, and even some children take part, all carrying red books of Mao's quotations.

102. *Scene from a modern ballet*: a newer expression of the class struggle. In this story, called "The White-haired Woman," the girl at right has risen up against her oppressor. Traces of China's classic theater linger on in both the makeup and stage setting.

103. *A girl student* ▶ (*overleaf*) of Peking University, China's finest school of higher learning, reads the familiar red book of Mao's sayings. Behind her, an old temple tower watches impartially, a solitary reminder of other days and dynasties.

149

THIS BEAUTIFUL WORLD